A Deeper Walk
in Marriage

Barry Chesney
Chuck McCammon
Cathy Napier

Statement:

I, ________________,

know that ______________

has my back in our marriage journey

and commitment to one another.

Table of Contents

Introduction

Men and women fall in love, sometimes quickly, and set a date for the wedding. They long to say "I do" at the altar before God and then begin their marriage journey. Do most couples have any idea what they have committed to? Probably not.

Couples meet, present the best version of themselves, and often get married quickly. Before long, couples learn that living together involves a major adjustment. Their best behavior starts to crumble. Most couples fail to consider that what they bring into the marriage can be from generations ago. The household they grew up in can have a positive or negative influence on them. They may be unaware that they're taking their family history into the marriage.

Let's look at Faye and George's marriage.

Faye was twenty-four and George was twenty-five when they fell in love and were married. After ten years of marriage and three children, life was fast-paced, and they rarely connected relationally. They realized that their arguments were more frequent and intense than when they first married.

Both claim they had accepted Christ in college while attending Campus

Crusade for Christ, but admitted the challenges of children, work, and general responsibilities kept them from regularly attending church or living a committed Christian life. They agreed it had been years since they opened or studied the Bible.

George was frustrated due to Faye's constant complaining that he never spent time with the family and that he was basically never home. George felt that Faye did not understand or appreciate his job commitment or the pressure he felt to provide for his family. Faye also wanted George to pick up some responsibility—to take their children to their various sports activities, for instance. But he stated that was impossible because he worked late most nights.

Both realized how far they had drifted apart, with little or no communication other than talking about their children. They never talked about what was going on in their lives, let alone how they were feeling mentally and emotionally. During one argument, George told Faye that she was drinking more than a glass of wine in the evening.

Faye complained that George wasn't affectionate, and George said that there was never any time for sex due to Faye's alcohol problem or her complaining about fatigue. Faye noticed George's anger escalating. George was known to have a quick temper, but lately, his anger had raised concern and caused her to fear for her safety.

Once, in the heat of an argument and a moment of high frustration, the word *divorce* came out of Faye's mouth. This was the first time the word had been spoken. Both admitted they had thought about divorce more than once but had never voiced it to the other. Faye confided in a Christian friend, who suggested the couple participate in a marriage ministry at a local church. Thankfully, they did.

In the ministry, Faye and George were reminded of the Gospel and the forgiveness they received from Jesus Christ. They discovered how to love each other through God's eyes. They learned humility, to disclose weaknesses, and to ask for forgiveness. They learned how to speak the truth in love, communicate clearly, and recommit to their marriage.

God blessed their time in the marriage ministry. It gave them the desire to pursue more discipleship-based marriage ministry. So, they signed up for another marriage ministry called *A Deeper Walk in Marriage*, written by Chuck McCammon, Barry Chesney, and Cathy Napier, of Valleydale Baptist Church in Birmingham, Alabama.

A Deeper Walk in Marriage takes a couple through a step-by-step approach that solidifies their marriage and enables them to practice daily exercises to keep their marriage alive. The exercises are integrated with God's word, so they and others continue to develop a Biblical worldview of marriage. With each exercise, a couple will follow Biblical principles of marriage that lead to oneness.

In *A Deeper Walk*, we begin by exploring the family of origin everyone brings into a marriage. Next, we identify outside influences—toxic relationships that can negatively impact a marriage. We teach you how to prevent infidelity, and how to find God's purpose for you and your family. We demonstrate how to trust in your relationship where it has been broken, and how to use conflict resolution to resolve disagreements quickly. Finally, we provide key insights on sexual intimacy, dealing with all addictions when applicable, and maintaining financial freedom.

Chapter 1:
Family of Origin

The author Philip Yancey wrote about a friend whose marriage was troubled. One night, the friend snapped and screamed at his wife, "I hate you! I won't take it anymore. I've had enough! I won't go on! I won't let it happen! No! No! No!"

Months passed. One night, the friend was awakened by sounds coming from his two-year-old son's room. He walked down the hall and stopped by the boy's door. What he heard sent shivers down his spine. Inside, his son was repeating in a soft voice—with precise inflection and intonation—the argument between his mother and father: "I hate you! ... I won't take it! ... No!"[1]

That story should give us chills because it is a sober reminder that words have consequences. The husband probably had no idea that his angry and hurtful words would later be repeated by his young son. Yet, what was at the root of the husband's hurt? Why was he yelling at his wife seemingly out of nowhere? In this chapter, we will explore the role played

---

1. Ortberg, John; *Everybody's Normal Until You Get to Know Them*, Zondervan, 2003, p. 166

by our family of origin, and we will discover that all of us are impacted by the families that raised us, whether we realize it or not.

Clearly, we received many good things from our families.[2] It may be our ability to work hard for a worthwhile goal, to handle finances, to have a sense of humor, and patience, or the ability to resist emotional drama. But our families can impact us in negative ways as well, and often the connection to the past is less obvious—to us, at least. We can adopt bad habits and patterns, or we can respond to negative events and behaviors in unhealthy ways.[3]

Could the two-year-old in Yancey's story fully grasp the meaning of what he was parroting? Likely not. However, the emotion, the tone, and the way these words were said are lasting. They can color his perspective and impact him in ways he may never understand.

For the purposes of this exercise, you will turn your focus to the hurt and negative patterns that have been in play in your family. Not because your family is responsible for your behavior, but because this exercise can shed light on ways your family has influenced you that you may not immediately recognize. Taking time to chart your past might reveal something to you that previously escaped your notice.[3]

Each person will use the blank genogram to look back at generations who have, either by genetic makeup or learned behavior, trickled down through multiple generations, wreaking havoc with your current marriage. The more detailed and invested you are in this project, the more likely it is that you will get helpful results. You may have to contact parents, and even grandparents to complete the genogram.

Put all emotional, mental, and addiction history in the blocks. For example, don't ignore depression, anxiety, trauma, or emotional regulation, such as anger, fear/phobia, etc. Also, please list any known addictions, such as alcoholism, drug addiction, gambling, sex addiction, eating

---

2. Proverbs 6:20-22

3. Colossians 3:21

disorders, etc.

Let's take the principle of the genogram and apply it to a family in the Bible. We will start with Joseph from the book of Genesis. We find him lying in a pit that his brothers violently tossed him into, leaving him for dead. Joseph was stunned and alarmed. He probably wondered if this was how he would die. As his young life flashed before him, he tried to figure out how he ended up in this situation, but he gained no understanding. He hadn't done anything to deserve this. He needed to dig deeper. A few generations deeper!

On two occasions, Abraham, Joseph's great-grandfather, chose to deceive his wife, Sarah.[4] Both times, Abraham and Sarah had traveled to a foreign land. Each time, Abraham feared that the leaders of these lands would find Sarah to be beautiful and desire her for themselves. Having no use for Abraham, these foreign leaders would kill him so that Sarah would be "available" to them. As each story unfolds, we see that Abraham's expectations of these foreign leaders were correct. However, Abraham's solution was to introduce Sarah to them as his sister rather than as his wife, thereby sparing his life. While this remedied Abraham's problem, it still put Sarah in jeopardy with these men. Each time, the deception was discovered, and Sarah was reunited with Abraham. But what cost had this deception brought to Sarah and to their marriage?

Fast forward a generation to Abraham and Sarah's son, Isaac. Isaac was married to Rebekah. Due to a famine, Isaac and Rebekah left home and settled in a foreign land. Isaac feared that since Rebekah was so beautiful the king would want to have her as his wife and would kill him to get her.[5] You can see where this is going. When Isaac made his introductions, he said, "My name is Isaac, and this is my . . . um . . . *sister*, Rebekah! Isn't that right, Sis?" (Wink, wink. Icy glare.)

It is crystal clear where Isaac picked up this strategy, right? As with

---

4. Genesis 12, 20

5. Genesis 26

his parents, once the deception was discovered, the couple was reunited. But unlike the Peaches & Herb song, being reunited didn't feel so good![6]

Fast forward another generation. Isaac was old and dying. His oldest son, Esau, was set to receive his father's blessing. While Esau was away, Isaac's other son, Jacob, used a stunning ruse to deceive his father into giving him the blessing meant for Esau.[7] Not only did Jacob inherit the art of deception from his ancestry—he also expanded the family business!

This time, two people conspired to deceive. Jacob was the frontman, but his mother assisted him behind the scenes. This deception took on an entirely new level of cunning, with a result so devastating that Esau promised to kill Jacob.[8] But not to be outdone, in the following generation, Jacob's sons hatched a deception that topped them all. They tossed their brother, Joseph, in a pit, and then told their father that a wild animal attacked and killed him![9]

A genogram will not prevent you from being tossed in a pit, but it may shine a light on how you got there! You will find your blank genogram on the following page.

---

6. Peaches & Herb, "Reunited", track 3 on *2 Hot*, 1979

7. Galatians 27:1-40

8. Genesis 27:41

9. Genesis 37:18-36

GENOGRAM

List the negative attributes you have inherited from your family of origin. Stick to areas of depression, anxiety, obsessive-compulsive behavior, attention deficit disorder, anger, and addictions (be specific and name the addictions.)

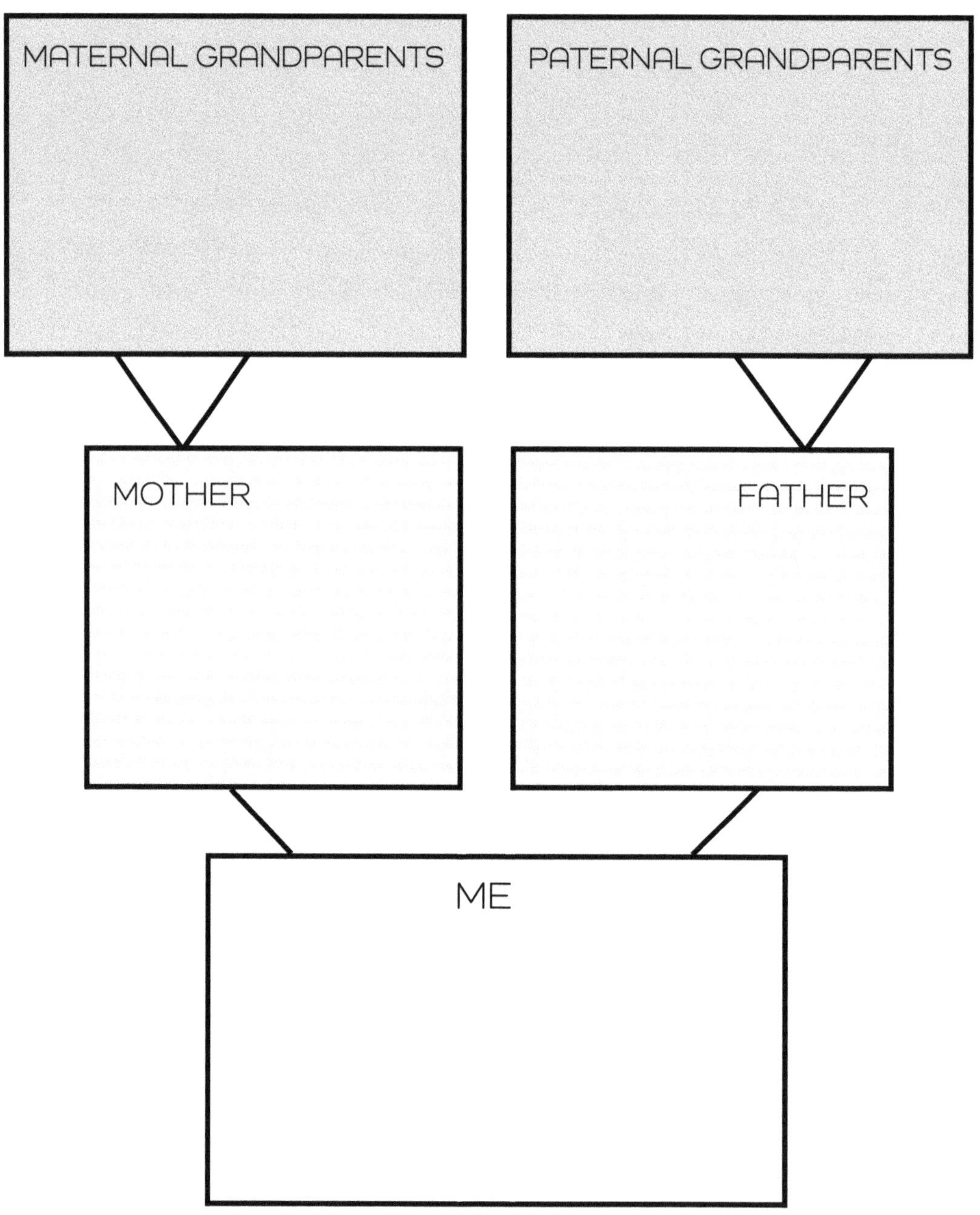

Use the space below to journal about the negative traits you feel you've brought into your marriage from your family of origin. Be ready to discuss these with the group. Become aware of triggering keywords from this list. Discuss with your spouse how you both can learn from this exercise and change the way you interact with one another.

Use the space below to describe your findings and your feelings about what you have discovered about your family of origin and the positive inherited traits you feel you have and how they have been good for your marriage.

Use the space below to write about your feelings when seeing the full picture of your past family. Summarize the negative and positive aspects of what you have discovered about yourself while doing these exercises. Please share the outcome with your spouse and the group.

____

____

____

____

____

____

____

Anger and shaming words can trigger an abnormal response during an argument. Can you identify words and actions that your spouse may say or do that cause a response from you due to what you have discovered in the genogram exercise?

____

____

____

____

____

____

____

____

JOURNALING PAGE

Chapter 2:
Marriage Purpose and Rebuilding Trust

God has a general and specific purpose for all believers. David wrote in Psalm 138, "The LORD will fulfill his purpose for me" (v.8a). God's first purpose for every Christian is to shape that person into the image of His Son, Jesus. Romans 8:29 says, "For those whom he foreknew he also predestined to be conformed to the image of his Son, in order that he might be the firstborn among many brothers."

We will ultimately be like Jesus when we see Him, whether He returns to earth during our lifetime or when we die and go to heaven. So, the Christian life is a process of becoming more like Jesus. One path that God uses to transform us is marriage.

In marriage, Bible study and prayer are two disciplines essential to spiritual growth. Couples need to read the Bible together daily as a family with their children, but also separately as a couple. Humans have more than a body; we have a soul, and the way we feed our soul is to commune with God. Read the Scriptures and spend time in prayer twice a day (or more if desired). For the couple, read and pray at bedtime. Or, if the morning works better, practice reading the Bible and praying together in the morning before the day's activities begin. Either way, this should be a quiet time for those with children.

God also has a specific purpose for a Christian's life and marriage.[10] He has a specific city where He wants us to live and a specific career for us. He has prepared people for us to reach for Christ.

Think for a moment about a man named Philip in Acts 8. Philip preached the gospel in Samaria to crowds of people (v. 6). People listened, demons were cast out, and the paralyzed or lame were healed. It appears that revival was taking place in Samaria through Philip's ministry. Verse 8 says there was much joy in that city. Yet, later in the chapter, an angel of the Lord said to Philip, "Rise, and go toward the south to the road that goes down from Jerusalem to Gaza" (v. 26). God instructed Philip to leave Samaria, where miracles occurred, and travel toward the remote area of Gaza. Gaza was the last place that water was available in southwestern Israel on the way to Egypt.[11]

Why would God call Philip to leave a thriving ministry? God had one person in mind to hear the gospel from Philip—an Ethiopian who was a court official of Candace (v. 27). This official had come to Jerusalem and was now traveling back home via the exact road to Gaza where God had sent Philip. The Ethiopian was reading in Isaiah and at that moment the Holy Spirit told Philip to go over to join that chariot (v. 29). The Ethiopian invited Philip to sit in his chariot, and given the passage he read from, Philip explained the Gospel to him and told him the good news about Jesus.

The Ethiopian decided it was time to get baptized and Philip had the privilege of baptizing him (v. 38). After Philip performed the baptism, the Holy Spirit took him away and placed him at Azotus, where he continued

---

10. A great example of a couple that lived on mission for God is Aquila and Priscilla, who Paul met in Corinth (see Acts 18).

11. Darrell L. Bock, *Acts* (Grand Rapids: Baker Academic, 2007), 341.

preaching the Gospel until he came to Caesarea (v. 40). Philip preached the Gospel everywhere that God took him. God had a specific purpose for Philip and specific people for whom to share the Gospel in specific places. God has specific plans for your life and marriage as well. The key is to daily surrender your will to Him and allow Him to direct your steps.

Ask the Lord to show you as a couple or individually what His plan is for your life. In faith, act on the plan that He reveals to you. The Lord will reveal His purpose to you in His timing. In the meantime, a great place to begin serving is in your local church. Take a step of faith and begin serving as a first impressions volunteer, or in ministry for those with special needs. Consider working with preschoolers or older children. Watch God work through you.

By volunteering for offered activities, you're discovering one way God will allow His purpose to manifest in your spiritual walk with Him. Ask Him and He will show you. Write answers to the following questions as you seek to discover God's will for your marriage:

1. Am I seeking God's purpose for my life and my family's life? What are examples of this?

2. Does my prayer life state to the Lord that I'm willing to do whatever He asks of me? Here's another way to think about this: are you spending time in prayer worshiping God, and asking Him to show you His will for you and your family?

3. What are my interests that God can use within the church?

Rebuilding Trust

How do you build trust when trust has been broken? In Psalm 9:10, David wrote, "And those who know your name put their trust in you, for you, O LORD, have not forsaken those who seek you." We can always trust

God because He is faithful and will never hurt us or turn His back on us.

People are different. People *can* hurt us. Even those who love us can walk out on us. Because we are sinners, we make mistakes, and sometimes those intentional or unintentional errors leave deep wounds in those we love. Trust can be broken in a marriage, due to lies, adultery, desertion, addiction (gambling, pornography, etc.), or workaholism. But if the spouse who broke trust and damaged the marriage is willing to stay married and work to repair trust, how do couples do that? What is the first step?

Please consider the following questions as a starting point:

1. What is the status of my Christian life right now? Am I living as holy a life as possible? If not, what can I change to reflect on my spouse that I'm living for Christ?

2. List the things that you know are a hindrance in your marriage. Ask yourself: What is my role in those hindrances?

3. List specific ways you can change these hindrances.

4. Ask your spouse to point out those things that are creating a chasm in your marriage. Please assure them they have the freedom to speak the truth in love.

How do we build trust again with one another, especially after one of us has committed adultery? In short, we must keep our eyes on God and ask Him to fill us with His love. God is forgiving. Yes, He does impose consequences for sin, but He also forgives and forgets about sin.

In Joel 1, God pronounced judgment upon His people because of their sins. God would cause Judah's agricultural economy to falter, and the people's gladness would dry up as well (Joel 1:12). Yet, despite God's judgment on Judah, Joel 2:12-14a notes that God invited His people to return to Him: "Yet even now, declares the LORD, return to me with all your heart, with fasting, with weeping, and with mourning; and rend your hearts and not your garments. Return to the LORD your God, for he is gracious and merciful, slow to anger, and abounding in steadfast love; and he relents over disaster. Who knows whether he will not turn and relent, and leave a blessing behind him?"

God would have mercy on His people if they would return to Him. If your marriage has experienced a loss of trust through adultery or in some other way, please ask God for His mercy and healing of your marriage. Ask Him to intervene and restore trust and a spirit of forgiveness. On our own, we are paralyzed and unable to move forward due to hurt, shame, betrayal, and sadness. But God is able; He can do all things. Luke 1:37 says, "For nothing will be impossible with God." Turn to God and allow Him to work.

Here are some practical steps to move forward as you wait upon the Lord to bring healing.

1. Make sure your spouse has full access to your phone.

2. Give information on what your plans are for the day.

3. Don't bring up past infidelities. Give the hurt to Jesus daily until it lessens. Let old wounds heal instead of agitating them.

4. Know that God has forgiven the adultery, and so should you.

5. Don't keep secrets.

6. Don't lie; always tell the truth, and go out of your way to be open.

JOURNALING PAGE

Use the space below to journal behaviors that your spouse is exhibiting that indicate you can trust again. What positive steps are you seeing in the behavior of your spouse?

Chapter 3:
Toxic Relationships

A toxic environment can interfere with your relationship.

Take a closer look at friends or family who may be unaware of the toxicity they're causing in your relationship. Make a list of those people and decide as a couple what would be best for everyone.

You may want to limit the time you spend with those family members who interfere negatively in your life. As for friends, you need God's wisdom on which ones to remain close to and which ones to distance yourselves from. At the same time, please avoid isolating yourselves as a couple. Everyone needs friends—*especially* couples. Marriage does not exempt people from experiencing loneliness. The tendency in our day is to isolate ourselves from others. You can put gas in your vehicle and make purchases at Target without ever interacting with anyone.

We spend time at work, cleaning the house, caring for the children, and surfing on social media. This leaves little time to develop authentic friendships. This is to our peril. Proverbs 18:1 says, "Whoever isolates himself seeks his own desire; he breaks out against all sound judgment." In Proverbs, we see the wise person contrasted with the wicked or the foolish person. The verse above indicates that the foolish person refrains from social relationships to pursue selfish aspirations.[12]

Notice the last part of the proverb, which explains that self-isolation is unwise. All of us need friendships. God Himself exists in a relationship as Father, Son, and Holy Spirit. Since we are created in His image, we, too, are made for relationships. Maintaining healthy friendships takes time and sacrifice, but it is worth it.

Each partner in a couple also needs a special friend from the same sex to confide in. But it must be a friend who will first honor the couple's marriage and their responsibility to it. Setting boundaries for friends and family members is wise, as they can (either intentionally or unintentionally) interfere with the marriage. Below are some principles for setting these boundaries.

1. Identify the issue and the person who interferes with the marriage. For example, it might be a friend who always wants more of your time, while you feel your time should be given instead to your marriage or your family. Or it might be a parent who is controlling and monopolizes your time by calling too often or dropping in for a visit without first checking your family's schedule. Remember, the marriage relationship is the primary relationship in a family. It is the husband and wife who are one flesh—*not* the husband and wife and child or parents/in-laws.[13]

2. Address the issue in a kind and non-shaming way. Be loving as you speak the truth. Ephesians 4:32 says, "Be kind to one another, tenderhearted, forgiving one another, as God in

---

12. Bruce K. Waltke, *The Book of Proverbs, Chapters 15-31* (Grand Rapids: Eerdmans, 2005), 69.

13. See Genesis 2:24.

Christ forgave you."

3. If the boundary is tested, say that you're spending time with your husband or wife. When the family doesn't have scheduled family time and you're free, *then* you and your friend or family member can plan a time for visits.

4. Continue these steps if the boundary continues to be tested. Then keep the boundary until the friend or family member accepts that your family time comes first.

Write in the space below examples of friends or family members who you feel will need these exercises. Write about ways you can handle the situation without hurting the people involved. Discuss these approaches with one another, especially if they apply to parents or other family members.

____

____

____

____

____

____

____

____

____

____

JOURNALING PAGE

Chapter 4:
Conflict Resolution

Relational conflict is part of life after man's fall into sin. Any married couple knows well that conflict is inevitable. In the Song of Solomon, the bride said, "Catch the foxes for us, the little foxes that spoil the vineyards, for our vineyards, are in blossom" (2:15). Conflict can spoil the vineyard of a wonderful marriage if not handled in the proper way. There are many little "foxes" that couples face, such as finances, parenting, wayward children, demanding careers, and health challenges that must be addressed in a Biblical way.

According to James 4, the source for our quarrels and fights is that we have a sinful nature inside of us that wants to be right all the time.[14] James said, "You desire and do not have, so you murder. You covet and cannot obtain, so you fight and quarrel. You do not have, because you do not ask."[15] Our sinful nature wants to be right and wants to have its way. When it is denied, we fume in frustration, and marital conflict can ensue.

---

14. James 4:1.

15. James 4:2.

Always work toward being emotionally literate so you can resolve your differences quickly instead of having them fester, which will only make the chasm between you larger. When we harbor anger toward one another, it leads to bitterness and puts up fences in our marriage. Fences create separation and isolation, two things that can severely damage a marriage.

According to God's word, it is possible to be angry and not sin. Ephesians 4:26 says to be angry and not sin. How do we respond when we are angry? Do we isolate ourselves and leave the house to spend the night somewhere else? Certainly, if the home has become a hostile situation and one spouse feels unsafe, then one night away is probably a great idea.

But there must be a better way to handle normal conflict within marriage. God's word says to make sure the conflict is time sensitive. The rest of verse 26 says, "Do not let the sun go down on your anger." The type of anger described in Ephesians 4 is a festering anger that is irritated.[16] The point is that when anger festers it only escalates and will eventually lead to an outburst, whether emotional or physical.[17] In order to avoid such outbursts, Paul exhorted the Ephesian Christians to pursue peace with the other party before the sun went down. Relational conflict is time sensitive. To sleep with a clear conscience, we must pursue peace[18] with our spouse. That will mean confessing sin and asking for forgiveness.

The book of James states the tongue can do more damage to a marriage than any other problem. The tongue can wound or heal a marriage. See James, Chapter 3, below.

James 3 (ESV): Taming the Tongue

Not many of you should become teachers, my brothers, for you know that we who teach will be judged with greater

---

16. Harold W. Hoehner, Ephesians: An Exegetical Commentary (Grand Rapids: Baker Academic, 2002), 622.

17. Ibid.

18. Romans 12:18.

strictness. ² For we all stumble in many ways. And if anyone does not stumble in what he says, he is a perfect man, able also to bridle his whole body. ³ If we put bits into the mouths of horses so that they obey us, we guide their whole bodies as well. ⁴ Look at the ships also: though they are so large and are driven by strong winds, they are guided by a very small rudder wherever the will of the pilot directs. ⁵ So also the tongue is a small member, yet it boasts of great things.

How great a forest is set ablaze by such a small fire! ⁶ And the tongue is a fire, a world of unrighteousness. The tongue is set among our members, staining the whole body, setting on fire the entire course of life,[a] and set on fire by hell.[b] ⁷ For every kind of beast and bird, of reptile and sea creature, can be tamed and has been tamed by mankind, ⁸ but no human being can tame the tongue. It is a restless evil, full of deadly poison. ⁹ With it we bless our Lord and Father, and with it we curse people who are made in the likeness of God. ¹⁰ From the same mouth come blessing and cursing. My brothers,[c] these things ought not to be so. ¹¹ Does a spring pour forth from the same opening both fresh and saltwater? ¹² Can a fig tree, my brothers, bear olives, or a grapevine produce figs? Neither can a salt pond yield fresh water.

By curbing the tongue, you can expect wisdom from above, as stated in verses 13 through 18.

¹³ Who is wise and understanding among you? By his good conduct let him show his works in the meekness of wisdom. ¹⁴ But if you have bitter jealousy and selfish ambition in your hearts, do not boast and be false to the truth. ¹⁵ This is not the wisdom that comes down from above, but is earthly, unspiritual, demonic. ¹⁶ For where

jealousy and selfish ambition exist, there will be disorder and every vile practice. [17] But the wisdom from above is first pure, then peaceable, gentle, open to reason, full of mercy and good fruits, impartial and sincere. [18] And a harvest of righteousness is sown in peace by those who make peace.

See the questions below. As you answer, think carefully about your ability to hurt or heal with what you say to your spouse, either in the heat of an argument or in a more routine context. Please examine the wounding words as well as the healing words.

1. List criticisms we use that damage a marriage. Give examples of these damaging words.

2. List positive attributes that you see in your spouse. Practice paying your spouse compliments from this list. This would be a good time to share with the group the reasons you daily thank God for him or her.

To move from conflict to a place of understanding and harmony, please consider the following steps put together by the University of Mississippi Counseling Center for navigating through conflict. These are good examples of what couples should do during arguments.

- Remain calm. If you remain calm, it will be more likely that others will consider your viewpoint. There are two relevant verses we should memorize. The first is Proverbs 15:1, which says, "A soft answer turns away wrath, but a harsh word stirs up anger." Speaking softly and lovingly can diffuse a situation that is quickly escalating. The second is Psalm 141:3, which says, "Set a guard, O LORD, over my mouth; keep watch over the door of my lips!" In the heat of the moment, this is a great prayer to voice silently to God. God will give us the supernatural grace to remain silent and seek to understand before seeking to be understood.

- Express feelings in words, not actions. Telling someone directly and honestly how you feel can be a very powerful form of communication. If you start to feel so angry or upset that you feel you may lose control, take a "time out" and do something to help yourself feel steadier: take a walk, do some deep breathing, or whatever works for you. Affirm to your partner that his or her perspective is important and that you want to be in the right frame of mind to listen.

- Be specific about what is bothering you. Vague complaints are hard to work with.

- Deal with one issue at a time. Don't introduce new topics until the one you've already introduced has been fully discussed.

- No "hitting below the belt." Attacking areas of personal

sensitivity creates an atmosphere of distrust, anger, and vulnerability.

- Avoid accusations. Accusations will cause others to defend themselves. Instead, talk about how someone's actions make you feel.

- Don't generalize. Avoid words like "never" or "always."

- Avoid "make-believe." Exaggerating or inventing a complaint or your feelings about it will prevent the real issue from surfacing. Stick with the facts and your honest feelings.

- Don't stockpile negativity—storing up grievances and hurt feelings over time is counterproductive. It's difficult to deal with old problems, and almost impossible when they are numerous. Try to deal with problems as they arise.

- Avoid clamming up. When one person becomes silent and stops responding to the other, frustration and anger can result. Positive results can only be attained with two-way communication.

- Establish common ground rules.

Continue with the questions for this chapter below.

3. Write a personal plan of action based on the University of Mississippi Counseling Center's conflict resolution guide—something you can implement when an argument ensues with your spouse. Practice this plan in your mind, so that when the argument happens, you are ready to deal with the conflict without damaging what the two of you have, which is a healthy relationship.

Remember not to bring up old problems that have long been dealt with. Always stay in the first-person point of view when describing a problem. For example, say, "*I feel hurt when you* __________." Don't refer to "you" when expressing a problem. Don't, for example, say, "*You are selfish when you* __________." Instead, say, "I feel we can work on not being selfish, giving ourselves more to the needs of our marriage instead of our own desires."

These examples of "fair fighting" will work, provided you follow the rules. If the argument ensues with neither of you being able to start a discussion, then one of you will have to call a timeout, so you can return to discuss later using our format. If one of you continues and the anger escalates, then you will have to set the boundary and walk out until the other calms down. Couples will have to agree on what rules work for them when the anger persists.

JOURNALING PAGE

Chapter 5:
Intimacy

When conflict is handled in a Biblical way, forgiveness is displayed often, and intimacy results. This requires couples to confront disagreements as they arise. You've set boundaries with the people who are toxic to your marriage. You are working toward the purpose you feel God has for you and your family, and you are working to rebuild trust if necessary. If it applies, then you have dealt with any infidelities in your marriage.

You've put in place exercises for fair fighting, so your disagreements don't damage the hard work you've achieved. Now it's time to enjoy what God has given every marriage—the sexual intimacy your marriage needs to make you one in the eyes of our Lord.

A good starting point is in Scripture. Yes, even this part of your marriage is under the umbrella and authority of Scripture. Scripture creates for us an expectation in your marriage relationship that presupposes sexual enjoyment and fulfillment. It describes how sex in marriage is intended to be enjoyed.

One thing we learn is from the second chapter of Genesis, shortly following the creation of man. It says, "Adam and his wife were both naked, and they felt no shame."[19] Pause for a moment to let that sink in. God's design was for you and your spouse to feel that level of confidence, comfort, lack of inhibition, and freedom in physical intimacy. No secrets, nothing hidden, nothing withheld, no anxieties, and no shame.[20] Just the freedom and availability only found in the oneness of marriage designed by God.

So, what happened? Why is it that sex for so many today brings shame and guilt instead of the joy and pleasure God intended? The short answer is *sin*. After Adam and Eve sinned against God in Genesis 3:6,[21] the very next verse says their eyes were opened and they knew they were naked. There was no problem with being naked before the couple sinned. But now the couple tried to hide their nakedness by sewing fig leaves into loincloths. They tried to hide from the presence of God.[22] Sin led to fear, shame, and separation from a holy God.

In the Song of Solomon, Solomon uses the word "love" many times. There are several Hebrew words for love, but the one used most often here is *dod*. According to the Hebrew lexicon, *dod* refers to a "boiling, intense preoccupation with a lover."[23] The Song of Solomon records the couple's dating relationship, marriage night, and early days as a couple. The couple displays attraction and admiration for each other, and because of these,

---

19. Genesis 2:25

20. In his book *God on Sex*, Danny Akin wrote, "Sex is good; it is God's gift. It should be enjoyed and enjoyed often. This good gift of God will find its fullest expression realized when a man and woman give themselves completely to each other in the marriage relationship" (3).

21. "So when the woman saw that the tree was good for food, and that it was a delight to the eyes, and that the tree was to be desired to make one wise, she took of its fruit and ate, and she also gave some to her husband who was with her, and he ate."

22. Genesis 3:8 says, "And they heard the sound of the LORD God walking in the garden in the cool of the day, and the man and his wife hid themselves from the presence of the LORD God among the trees of the garden."

23. Old Testament Hebrew Lexical Dictionary developed by Jeff Garrison for Study-Light.org. Copyright 1999-2023.

their relationship thrives.[24] At the end of chapter four, the bride invites her husband to make love to her; "Let my beloved come to his garden," she says, "and eat its choicest fruit" (4:16b).[25] The couple has remained sexually pure and now it is time to enjoy sex as God created it.

God is for sex. He created it and intended it to be enjoyed in the confines of marriage. He is for you to find pleasure and enjoyment with your spouse. So, how do you get there? What do you need to know?

Steps to Enjoying the Marriage Bed

(Note: These steps take place well before the act of sex begins.)

1. *The first step is to build trust with your spouse.* If your spouse can trust you outside the bedroom, then it will be easier for them to trust you within the bedroom. Does your spouse know that you have their best interest at heart? Is your spouse confident that you want their good as much as, or even more than, your own? The greatest way you build trust is to say what you mean and mean what you say, and then let your actions back that up—consistently, over time.

2. *Communicate openly and honestly with your spouse.* Define your expectations for intimacy. Talk about what you like and dislike. Identify your needs and desires for intimacy. You will both learn a great deal about one another, and effective communication will help you be on the same page.

---

24. In 1:15, the man says, "Behold, you are beautiful, my love; behold, you are beautiful; your eyes are doves." In the very next verse (16), the woman says, "Behold, you are beautiful, my beloved, truly delightful."

25. Akin added, "She has been listening to every word spoken by her husband, for she picks up on the imagery of the garden. She is that garden, and her love is welcome to come in and enjoy. She invites him, she guides him, she tells him what she is feeling and what she wants. Great sex is the result of good communication." (*God on Sex*, 151.)

3. *Keep short accounts.* Throughout the day, every day, little things will happen—a poorly considered word here, a sideways glance there, an instant reaction that riles something in you. Most of these interactions are small, but they can douse the flame of intimacy quickly. Learn to overlook minor offenses and learn to forgive larger ones.[26] This way, the relational runway is clear for takeoff toward intimacy.

4. *Show affection in non-sexual ways.* Doing so helps your spouse sense that you are thinking about them in a warm and caring way. It fosters the trust spoken of earlier, and it lowers any negative emotions or feelings that may be brewing but have not yet surfaced. Also, showing physical affection in other ways makes the transition to sex seem like less of a leap.

5. *Make time to be intimate.* We lead busy lives. Our calendars are filled to the max. Any spare time is at the end of the evening, and by then we are tired and have no energy for sex or intimacy. You do not want to eliminate spontaneity from your repertoire, but sometimes it's good to *plan* sex. Set aside a night and time dedicated to being intimate. When planned, it can be something you look forward to, which can heighten the anticipation. The idea is to make time for what is important, and being intimate with your spouse is a highly important part of your marriage.

---

26. Proverbs 19:11

6. *Sex in marriage needs to be a regular occurrence.*[27] Sex does not have to be on a schedule, but regular sex has been scientifically proven to have many physical benefits. In addition, God designed chemicals to be released in our brains when we are intimate: oxytocin, dopamine, and vasopressin.[28] These chemicals are not only addictive, but they also release stress and help smooth some of the rough edges that can hinder our relationship with our spouse.

Questions for Reflection

1. How is your trust level with your spouse? Do you sense they have your best interests in mind? If not, what conversation(s) do you need to have?

2. What do you wish your spouse knew about your desires and expectations for intimacy? Have you expressed these desires and expectations to your spouse? If not, how could you initiate that conversation?

3. Is there anything between you and your spouse that is blocking the path toward intimacy? If so, are you able to overlook an offense or forgive as necessary?

Action Step: Talk to your spouse and schedule a time in the next week when you will clear the calendar and set aside time to be intimate with each other.

---

27. 1 Corinthians 7:5

28. Robinson, K.M. (2022, March 6). "10 Surprising Health Benefits of Sex." *Web MD.* https://www.webmd.com/sex-relationships/guide/sex-and-health

JOURNALING PAGE

Chapter 6:
Regaining Lost Intimacy

Taking a deeper walk into your marriage will solidify your union as a couple and enable you to have an active sex life again. Sex between married couples helps each partner forget and forgive the old hurts—the sorts of things you worked on in chapters 2 and 4, by participating in a deeper marriage engagement. This section is only to be shared within the couple and isn't for disclosure to anyone else.

Sexual intimacy is not just a gift from God, but it comes highly encouraged by God. God says to the married couple, "Let your wife be a fountain of blessing for you. Rejoice in the wife of your youth. She is a loving deer, a graceful doe. Let her breasts satisfy you always. May you always be captivated by her love."[29] Sexual intimacy is a blessing. However, it requires effort to achieve it as well as sustain it through the day-to-day rigors of marriage.

Previously in this study, we looked at Joseph, and saw in the book of Genesis how he was impacted by the sins of his ancestors. We traced his

---

29. Proverbs 5:18-19

problems back several generations to Abraham and Sarah. Their marriage was the stuff of soap operas. The events, as told in Genesis, must have had a negative impact on Abraham and Sarah's sexual intimacy.

What happened? On two separate occasions, Abraham made Sarah sexually available to a king rather than stand up and claim her as his wife, for fear that doing so would place his life in jeopardy with the rulers.[30] In addition, the couple struggled with Sarah's inability to have children.[31] Due to her infertility, Sarah offered her servant, Hagar, to Abraham for him to lie with and conceive a child.[32] But once Hagar became pregnant by Abraham, an intense rivalry formed between Hagar and Sarah.[33]

There was enough here to destroy any marriage. One need not be Sherlock Holmes to see the dagger that had been thrust into what had once been Abraham and Sarah's sexual intimacy.

Yet, despite all this, Abraham and Sarah must have been able to work through it, because eventually, they did conceive a son.[34] And the chain of descendants began, who ultimately became the nation of Israel. God's promise to forge a great nation from Abraham's innumerable descendants hinged upon Abraham and Sarah's ability to restore a level of sexual intimacy to their marriage. Certainly, God could have worked His plan without their involvement, but you get the point. If Abraham and Sarah could overcome all their marital issues to achieve sexual intimacy, then there is hope for your marriage as well.

A couple's intimacy can be interrupted by arguments, addictions, infidelity, depression, and other things.[35] The longer a couple stays out

---

30. Genesis 12, 20

31. Genesis 16:1a

32. Genesis 16:2

33. Genesis 16:4

34. Genesis 21:1-2

35. In his book *Life on the Edge: A Young Adult's Guide to a Meaningful Future*, James Dobson

of the marriage bed, the harder it is to get their sex life active again. But your life does not have to be a soap opera to have challenges with sexual intimacy. *Every* couple has intimacy issues within the marriage. The challenge begins with the mental aspect of sexual intimacy.[36] What you think about sexual intimacy, how you view it, the value you place on it, and the place you have reserved for it in your marriage will affect your pursuit of and engagement in sexual intimacy. And because you and your spouse are unique individuals with different backgrounds, experiences, and families of origin—not to mention the differences between males and females—under the best circumstances, you and your spouse are starting from two very different places with how you approach sexual intimacy.

So, it is necessary to engage your spouse in conversation to surface your thoughts, attitudes, and assumptions about sexual intimacy so that you can move from where you are on the spectrum toward oneness.[37] This is the part of the study where you discuss your sex life. Start by discussing what you feel you're going to need in the marriage bed. The steps below can give you some ideas:

1. Start a discussion on ways you can get back into routine sexual activity. Try to identify any barriers that have prevented you from engaging in regular sexual activity. Recognize and talk about when your sex life became less

---

wrote, "Remember that pornography is dangerous. It can warp the mind and destroy sexual intimacy in marriage. Stay away from it. A monster is crouched behind that door."

36. Capri (2022, June 28). *The Connection Between Mental Health and Intimacy.* Resources to Recover. https://www.rtor.org/2019/06/28/mental-health-and-intimacy/ Web article states, "While most of us assume that intimacy is something we only experience physically, intimacy also depends on, and greatly impacts, our brains. In fact, mental wellbeing and intimacy are so closely related that each can affect the other."

37. In his book *5 Essentials for Lifelong Intimacy,* James Dobson wrote, "This fiery, romantic, sexually intimate love is not achieved overnight. It develops between a man and woman through a process called marital bonding. Such bonding refers to the emotional covenant that links a man and woman together for life and makes them intensely valuable to one another."

active or non-existent. Verbalize a way you can become sexually active again.

2. State what you want out of sexual intimacy. Detail your requests. Couples often become embarrassed or shy about the details of what they need from their partner. It's time to start putting those feelings aside and work to obtain a comfortable sexual experience that God has ordained.

3. At the same time, state what you *don't* want. To be clear about what you want is also to articulate what you don't want or can't tolerate in your sex life.

4. Plan date nights if you have children. Going out once a week or planning alone time once a week is healthy for your marriage, especially if you have children. Regular times of dating and actively courting each other will have a tremendous and positive impact on your marriage.

5. If you don't have children, or if they are grown and out of the house, then be spontaneous. Work at being playful and affectionate with one another more often; ideally, every day.

6. Never let a day pass that you're not acknowledging your partner in small ways. For example, kiss, hold hands, touch, and genuinely complement one another. Work to keep from being critical of one another.

7. Each partner should help the other with personal business, work, or other demands, such as housework, running errands, and caring for the children. You know what must be done to make your family and household function, so

make sure you divide up the work evenly. That way, no one is too tired to engage in sexual activity.

8. Be kind and resolve arguments quickly. Arguments and disagreements are common when two people live together. But always refer to the fair fighting steps in the conflict resolution section of this workbook (Chapter 4).

If problems still come up after you've tried the above, then you should see a certified sex therapist who is also a Christian. There are several who are listed with Better Health and are certified Christian sex therapists.

JOURNALING PAGES

Blank pages for your personal journaling on this subject. Write down your positive feelings and the changes you are experiencing because of re-connecting with your spouse. For your eyes only!

____

____

____

____

____

____

____

____

____

Chapter 7:
Infidelity Prevention

In Genesis 39, we see a classic example of how to avoid sexual immorality.

The main characters in this story were Potiphar, Joseph, and Potiphar's wife (whose name we do not know). Joseph lived in an unwanted place. He grew up in the land of Canaan, where he had eleven brothers. Driven by jealousy, Joseph's brothers threw him into an empty pit, hoping to never see him again (Gen. 37:11,24).

Joseph was sold to the Ishmaelites for 20 shekels of silver and taken to Egypt. Joseph's brothers probably thought they would never see him again. Once in Egypt, Potiphar, an officer of Pharaoh and the captain of the guard, purchased Joseph from the Ishmaelites. What would Joseph's future hold in an unfamiliar land? Little did Joseph know that he would soon be confronted with sexual temptation. Joseph did not plan to be in Egypt, nor did he choose the sexual invitation posed by Potiphar's wife. But that is often the case with sexual temptation; it is sneaky and subtle, and it will destroy our lives if we succumb to it. If you interviewed a husband or wife who engaged in sexual infidelity, he or she would probably tell you they did not plan for it to occur. They did not intend to ruin their lives.

Rather, they found themselves in an unwanted place where they were confronted with sexual temptation, and they made the wrong choice.

So, how can we avoid infidelity in our marriages? How can we remain pure, as Joseph did in this chapter? Admittedly, Joseph was single and not married, but his character in Genesis 39 is spotless, and we can learn from his example.

Joseph was an interesting man. Each year, *People Magazine* names "the sexiest man alive," and if this periodical had existed in Joseph's day, perhaps he would have been on the cover. Joseph had six positive traits that made him desirable, and there were six things that he did to avoid sexual infidelity. Let's pay close attention and learn from Joseph.

First, Joseph was successful. Genesis 39:2 says that the LORD was with Joseph, and he became a successful man. The Hebrew reads "and he was a prosperous man," which does not refer to wealth, but that he made progress in all that he did. The theological point here is that God was at work in Joseph's life outside the land of Canaan—that is, outside the land of blessing that God had promised to Abram. God did not let Joseph's transfer to Egypt ruin his life. Behind the scenes, God was at work and sent Joseph on ahead so that He could establish the Hebrew people in Egypt. Of course, Joseph did not know any of this yet.

Second, Joseph was highly regarded by others. Joseph's master saw that God was with him and that the LORD caused all that he did to succeed in his hands (v.3). When God is at work in someone's life, people notice. For example, at the end of 1 Samuel 3, we see that young Samuel grew up, and the LORD was with him and let none of his words fall to the ground (v.19). Whatever Samuel said, it came true. Verse 20 says that all of Israel, from Dan to Beersheba, knew that Samuel was established as a prophet of the LORD. The phrase "from Dan to Beersheba" was a way of saying from the northern point of Israel to the southern border. The entire country recognized that Samuel was a prophet of the LORD. He did not have to promote himself to Israel that he was a man of God. Everyone knew it. Likewise, Joseph did not have to walk around Potiphar's house talking about how spiritual he was. It was evident. God's hand was on his life and Joseph's master took notice. And we believe Potiphar's wife took notice, too—but more on that later.

Third, Joseph had status. Verse 4 says that Joseph's master made him overseer of his house and put him in charge of all that he had. In other words, Joseph's master "put into his hand" everything he had. Joseph had been sold as a slave, but he no longer retained that status. He had moved up the social ladder. Joseph had a position of authority now in Egypt and in Potiphar's house. That may have evoked jealousy in some who worked under him, but it aroused admiration in others—namely Potiphar's wife. Either way, because of God's favor, Joseph rose through the social ranks in Egypt, and people took notice.

Fourth, Joseph had power. The ESV translation uses the term "overseer" for Joseph's position in verse 5. As soon as Joseph was promoted to overseer in Potiphar's house, God's hand of blessing was on all the Egyptians. Verse 6 says that Joseph's master left all that he had in Joseph's charge. The only thing his master concerned himself with was the food he ate. Everything else was under Joseph's watch. Joseph had the position, the power, and the admiration. He had a lot going for him. However, positions of power often lead to great temptation. Joseph's sexual invitation would come from an admirer who had been paying attention to his distinguished reputation.

Fifth, Joseph was dependable. Joseph's master left everything in Joseph's charge. Apparently, Joseph handled it very well because his master lived without concern. Joseph showed up to work on time, perhaps even early, and probably stayed late to make sure he finished the job. Joseph could handle the responsibility; he had not been promoted beyond his competency.

Sixth, Joseph had good looks. He was a handsome young man. The last part of verse 6 says that he was handsome in form and appearance. This description of Joseph's physical traits is unusual for a male in Scripture but is included to help explain the sinful behavior of Potiphar's wife in the next scene. The NET Bible translation says that Joseph was "well-built and good-looking." Joseph was blessed with good looks and Potiphar's wife took notice.

These six traits reflect God's blessing on Joseph's life, and they speak of Joseph's godly character. But they also made Joseph a target for a sexual invitation. We need to learn from this. Your success at your job, your physical attractiveness, and your respectability in the community are great attributes, but they can also be alluring to another person. We had better pay attention to how Joseph handled a sexual advance so that we know how to correctly deal with it.

Notice that in verse 7 it says that "after a time his master's wife cast her eyes on Joseph." We do not know exactly how much time has elapsed. Perhaps it was a couple of weeks. Or it could have been a few months. Either way, during that time Joseph had distinguished himself. Perhaps Potiphar bragged about Joseph to his wife, praising his ability and his positive attitude. She began to esteem Joseph highly and when she laid eyes on him, she was attracted to him. Maybe she was even attracted to his accent, given that he was not from Egypt.

The phrase "after a time" means that during this period, internal passions for Joseph escalated in the heart of Potiphar's wife. Attraction led to arousal, and she approached Joseph, inviting him to have sex with her. She said, "Lie with me." In Hebrew, this is a two-word expression that is never used in the context of marriage. It indicates uncivilized lust. Potiphar's wife's invitation was direct and aggressive, and it anticipated immediate fulfillment.

How did Joseph respond? He refused her sexual advance, saying, "Behold, because of me my master has no concern about anything in the house, and he has put everything that he has in my charge." Notice that Joseph could have said "your husband," but instead he referred to Potiphar as "my master." Joseph respected the authority God had placed him under and would not circumvent it.

There are six qualities that Joseph had that helped him avoid sexual immorality. The first was perspective. Joseph did not succumb to temptation in the heat of the moment but instead had the perspective to see the situation for what it was; the danger that could destroy his life. Joseph's master trusted him. By sleeping with his wife, Joseph would have betrayed that trust and lost everything. Oh, the beauty of having perspective! How many people end up in sexual immorality because of lost perspective? They get enthralled with a person or with sexual fantasies, and they forget that sexual sin could cause them to lose their jobs, their intimate fellowship with Jesus, their reputation, and most likely their families. But not Joseph; he had the wherewithal to think about what was at stake.

Second, Joseph respected limits. In verse 9, he said that his master had not withheld anything from him except his wife. Joseph knew the boundary, and he respected it. There was a limit to his authority in Potiphar's house, and he would not exceed that limit. It is interesting that from the Garden of Eve until today, many people have seen limits as a source of frustration. But Joseph saw his limits as a reason for loyalty to his master.

We live in an era when many people refuse to acknowledge and respect the limits or boundaries that God has set in place. In his book *Strange New World*, Carl Trueman talks about expressive individualism, which says that each person has a unique internal feeling or instinct that should be expressed if that person's individuality is to be realized[38]. Philosopher Charles Taylor, the author of *A Secular Age*, calls expressive individualism a "culture of authenticity," where living authentically means acting upon our feelings. In other words, our society says we are "authentic" when we express outwardly what we feel inwardly.

That is scary, because we can feel many things inwardly, and many of them are sinful. When we act upon the sinful desires we have in our hearts, it is not "authentic"; according to Scripture, it is sinful. Joseph recognized that God placed limits on humanity, and one of those limits was not having sex with another man's wife. Joseph respected that limit and refused to accept Potiphar's wife's invitation.

---

38. Carl Trueman, *Strange New World: How Thinkers and Activists Redefined Identity and Sparked the Sexual Revolution.* Wheaton, IL: Crossway, 2022.

Third, Joseph feared God. He asked Potiphar's wife a question at the end of verse 9 that demonstrated this fear; "How then can I do this great wickedness and sin against God?" There are two key components to this question. First, Joseph viewed sin as great wickedness. Sexual immorality is a sin, and it is great wickedness. The phrase "great wickedness" highlighted the moral depravity of Potiphar's wife's invitation to Joseph. It was not simply a physical act, free of implications. It was not casual sex designed to satisfy both partners. It was wrong and wicked. Because Joseph feared God, he saw sin for what it was: wickedness. Joseph still feared God, even though he had endured extreme mistreatment from his own brothers. He had not turned his back on God, even though we wonder if he ever questioned if God had forgotten him as he was being transported to Egypt and away from his father.

The second component of Joseph's question is that he saw sin as primarily an offense against God. Sin hurts people, but ultimately it offends God because it breaks His law. God designed sex to be enjoyed in the marriage bed, and any sex outside of this design is a sin. King David, who committed sexual sin, confessed in Psalm 51 that sin is ultimately committed against God (v.4). In Deuteronomy 22, laws against sexual immorality were communicated to Israel, and in verse 22 of this chapter, it says that if a man is found lying with the wife of another man, both of them shall die so that the evil is purged from Israel. Sexual sin is serious. Joseph understood that, and he refused to participate.

Fourth, Joseph persevered. Notice in verse 10 that Potiphar's wife had persistence; "And as she spoke to Joseph day after day." Sexual temptation is not a one-time occurrence. Joseph worked in Potiphar's house, and at this point in the story, Potiphar's wife would not accept "no" for an answer. She knew where to find Joseph and kept approaching him, hoping she would catch him in a moment of weakness, and he would finally accept her invitation. But Joseph would not listen to her; he tuned out her voice and sexual advances.

Fifth, Joseph imposed boundaries in his life. The end of verse 10 says that he would not listen to, lie beside, or be with Potiphar's wife. Joseph recognized that he could not be alone with her and he had to impose protective measures to guard his moral integrity. When we teach people how to drive, we often tell them they will have to drive defensively, meaning they must watch out for other drivers who may not be paying attention. Avoiding sexual immorality requires us to live defensively.

We must be proactive and set boundaries in our lives that protect us from situations where sexual advances could occur. It is hard to have an adulterous affair with a member of the opposite sex if you have a rule of not being alone with a member of the opposite sex outside of the family. If you are texting a person of the opposite sex, consider including your spouse on the text thread so he or she is aware of the conversation. That way, nothing is hidden. Avoid riding alone in a vehicle with a person of the opposite sex. Solomon instructed his son in Proverbs 5:8 on the importance of avoiding the adulterous woman; "Keep your way far from her, and do not go near the door of her house." Of course, the same principle applies to a woman who needs to avoid a man who is pursuing her. The point is that defensive boundaries are essential if we are going to remain morally pure in a culture enamored with sex.

The sixth and final quality in Joseph's life that helped him avoid sexual immorality was that he knew when to run. Joseph went into the house one day to do his work, and Potiphar's wife intensified her sexual advance. Previously, she had spoken to Joseph, but now she grabbed him (v.12a) and said, "Lie with me." For Joseph, all bets were off, so he removed himself from the situation. Verse 12 says, "But he left his garment in her hand and fled and got out of the house." Joseph knew when to leave. It was an ambush, and Joseph knew it, so he ran. Paul wrote in 1 Corinthians 6:18, "Flee from sexual immorality." Don't flirt with it. Run away from it. In doing so, you can remain pure before the Lord and protect your spouse from severe hurt.

In our culture, it is hard for men and women to be separated in the workplace, so it's easy to find themselves involved in an extramarital affair. But for as long as men and women have worked together in the corporate world, there have been numerous affairs and an increase in divorce. Women entering the workforce is not the only cause of divorce but has become a major one.

Proverbs 5 includes a good description of the archetype of the adulterous woman.

Proverbs 5

My son, pay attention to my wisdom, listen well to my words of insight, that you may maintain discretion and your lips may preserve knowledge. For the lips of an adulteress drip honey, and her speech is smoother than oil; but in the end, she is bitter as gall, sharp as a double-edged sword. Her feet go down to death; her steps lead straight to the grave. She gives no thought to life; her paths are crooked, but she knows it not. Now listen my sons, listen to me; do not turn aside from what I say. Keep to a path far from her, do not go near the door of her house, lest you give your best strength to others and your years to one who is cruel, lest strangers feast on your wealth and your toil enrich another man's house. At the end of your life, you will groan, when your flesh and body are spent. You will say, "How I hated discipline! How my heart spurned correction! I would not obey my teachers or listen to my instructors. I have come to the brink of utter ruin in the midst of the whole assembly." Drink water from your own cistern, running water from your own well. Should your springs overflow in the streets, your streams of water in the public squares? Let them be yours alone, never to be shared with strangers. May your fountain be blessed and may you rejoice in the wife of your youth. A loving doe, a graceful deer—may her breasts satisfy you always, and may you ever be captivated by her love. Why be captivated, my son, by an adulteress? Why embrace the bosom of another man's wife? Man's ways are in full view of the Lord, and he examines all his paths. The evil deeds of a wicked man ensnare him; the cords of his sin hold him fast. He will die from lack of discipline, led astray by his own folly.

In modern times, this archetype of the adulterous woman has been described by the DSM-5-TR (the *Diagnostic and Statistical Manual for Mental Illnesses*). But although the proverb is describing a woman, a man can have the same characteristics. The DSM-5-TR describes the woman or man who sets their sights on a married man or woman (with or without children), and notes that they can exhibit symptoms of a narcissistic personality. Proverbs describe her with a mouth that flatters and drips sweetness like honey. But men can have a mouth that flatters, too, and that also drips with the sweetness of honey.

Here are some of the symptoms of a narcissistic personality:

1. A preoccupation with fantasies of unlimited success, power, brilliance, beauty, or ideal love.

2. A need for excessive admiration. A narcissistic person can never get enough love and attention.

3. A sense of entitlement. Narcissistic person feels they deserve to have as many affairs as they choose to have.

4. Interpersonal exploitive behavior. This means using someone unfairly—for instance, for sex.

5. A lack of empathy. A narcissistic person does not consider who may get hurt in their relationships.

When men or women become taken in by the charms of a narcissist, they lose the ability to simply walk away. Involvement with the narcissist becomes a trap—like the female black widow spider, who has sex with her male counterpart, and then eats him.

Here is a protocol to help you avoid involvement with a woman or man who is overly friendly and has made clear that they want an adulterous relationship:

1. Tell her or him you're married and will uphold your marriage vows

2. If possible, distance yourself

3. Inform your wife or husband of the situation

4. Don't be alone with her or him

5. If the woman or man persists, tell your wife or husband to give her or him a call or text

Discussion Questions:

1. 1 Corinthians 6:18 says, "Flee from sexual immorality." Discuss with your spouse the situations in your life where sexual immorality could rear its ugly head. Define specific ways to flee from those situations.

2. Sexual immorality can cause great devastation to a person's life and especially to a marriage. List as many things as you can think of that could be lost or damaged because of sexual immorality.

3. Read 1 Thessalonians 4:4. Sexual immorality doesn't "just happen." There is usually a buildup of flirtation, fantasy, and opportunity that occurs over time. According to this passage, resisting temptation is a

form of self-control. But our spouse is our helper—given to us to strengthen us in all things, even self-control. Discuss with your spouse any shared language you can create to help you keep one another accountable.

4. In the Genesis account, Joseph was able to resist the temptations presented by Potiphar's wife due in part to the fact that he had established some clear boundaries prior to the temptation. What are some healthy boundaries you could establish and implement? How can your spouse support you in maintaining those boundaries?

5. Prayer is an important weapon in the arsenal against immorality. It's like the glue that holds marriages together. Spend a few moments in prayer for one another, to help you each avoid, flee, and escape from sexual immorality.

JOURNALING PAGE

Chapter 8:
Addictive Behavior

Address all addictions that you're holding on to.

Addictions will destroy an individual and a family unit faster than anything else. A husband or wife who struggles with alcoholism or drug addiction presents a false sense of who they are to their partner. The addicted husband or wife is always having a relationship with the chemical. The person they married and fell in love with has disappeared. Loneliness sets in.

Unless removed from the family unit, alcoholism and drug addiction always win. Alcohol or drug addiction takes the relationship, the time spent with children, the sexual intimacy, the money, the home, the health, and eventually the person's life, unless they get into recovery.

As Christians, how can we lovingly help someone addicted to alcohol? Does the Bible have anything to say about alcohol consumption or abuse?[39]

---

39. For a very helpful article on wine as it appears in the Bible see Robert H. Stein, "Wine Drinking in New Testament Times," *Christianity Today*, June 20, 1975. Retrieved from https://www.christianitytoday.com/ct/1975/june-20/wine-drinking-in-new-testament-times.html on June 1, 2022. Stein argued there is a significant difference in the wine of New Testament times and the wine consumed today. Wine in New Testament times

It absolutely does.[40]

First, the Scriptures clearly prohibit the abuse of alcohol among Christians and especially spiritual leaders.[41] In Ephesians 5:18, Paul wrote, "And do not get drunk with wine, for that is debauchery, but be filled with the Spirit." Proverbs 20:1 also presents alcohol abuse in a negative light by saying, "Wine is a mocker, strong drink a brawler, and whoever is led astray by it is not wise." The NASB translation says, "And whoever is intoxicated by it is not wise."

In describing qualifications for the spiritual leadership of elders and deacons in the church, Paul said an elder must not be "a drunkard" (1 Tim. 3:3), a deacon must not be "addicted to much wine" (1 Tim. 3:8), and older women must not be "slaves too much wine" (Titus 2:3). There are many other Scriptures that also prohibit the abuse of alcohol.[42]

---

was heavily mixed with water compared to today's wine which has a much higher alcohol content.

40. The two most common words in the Old Testament that are used for alcohol are *shekar* (strong drink) and *yayin* (wine). These two words appear together as in Proverbs 20:1 above 21 times in the Old Testament. The word for strong drink refers to beer or any alcoholic beverage created from grain or fruit. The verbal form of this word, *shakar*, which means to be drunk or intoxicated, is used nearly 60 times in the Old Testament and only 5 of the uses refer to something good or acceptable. The few times shakar refers to something good it does not normally refer to someone consuming alcohol. For example, in Genesis 43:34 Joseph's brothers were with Joseph in Egypt and they drank and became drunk with him. The point here is not that they drank to intoxication but they were reunited and enjoyed each other's friendly company. Strong drink was used in the drink offering as seen in Numbers 28:7 but this does not refer to personal intoxication since worship was the goal of the offering. Proverbs 31:6 says to give strong drink to the one who is perishing, which presumably served a medicinal purpose offering temporary relief from pain. Taken from *Theological Wordbook of the Old Testament*, vol. 2, Harris, Archer, and Waltke, eds. (Chicago: Moody Press, 1980), 926-927. The term for wine (yayin) is used 140 times in the Old Testament for a drink at celebratory events and for use in offerings. Priests were forbidden to drink wine while they were ministering at the Tent of Meeting in Leviticus 10. Wine was a very intoxicating drink and probably contained about 7-10% alcohol content. Taken from *Theological Wordbook of the Old Testament*, vol. 1, Harris, Archer, and Waltke, eds. (Chicago: Moody Press, 1980), 865.

41. A spiritual leader must not be a drunkard (Titus 1:7, 1 Timothy 3:3).

42. Daniel B. Wallace, "The Bible and Alcohol," published June 21, 2004. Retrieved from

Second, consider the Scriptures where wine was part of celebratory events. In Genesis 14, Melchizedek brought out bread and wine to Abram (v.18). Job's children ate and drank wine together (Job 1:13). In Nehemiah 2:1, Nehemiah was a cupbearer to the king, and his job included tasting wine presented to the king. Psalm 104:14-15 describes God as the One who causes the grass to grow, so food and wine will spring from the earth to gladden the heart of man.

By now, the reader may be thinking, "Well, if God created wine and everything God created is good, then I can enjoy it whenever I want." That perspective should be tempered by our third point, which is that Scripture limits the Christian's freedom in order to promote spiritual growth. In Romans 14, Paul wrote about causing other Christians to stumble spiritually. "Stumbling" refers to placing an object in someone else's path that causes them to misstep and experience a spiritual plateau or even decline. One stumbling block presented in Scripture is alcohol. Paul wrote, "It is good not to eat meat or drink wine or do anything that causes your brother to stumble" (v.21). Paul's point is to pursue the spiritual edification of another Christian and avoid anything that gets in the way of that, even alcohol. A Christian may want to avoid it, especially if a younger brother or sister in the faith is near and might stumble because of it.

Some Christians may choose to drink alcohol in private to prevent another from stumbling. Some may choose to abstain from alcohol altogether. They would not be the first. In the Old Testament era, a group called the Nazirites took a vow that included abstaining from alcohol (Numbers 6:3-4). In the New Testament, John the Baptist, who foretold the ministry of Jesus, did not drink any wine (Luke 7:33).

While we cannot argue the Bible prohibits alcohol consumption for Christians, we can say it prevents *abuse* of alcohol. And in terms of whether Christians drink at all, we should give careful thought to the

---

https://bible.org/article/bible-and-alcohol on May 31, 2022. Other Scriptures that either prohibit alcohol abuse or present alcohol abuse in a negative light are Proverbs 21:17, 1 Samuel 1:14, Isaiah 5:11, 22, 28:1, Jeremiah 23:9, 51:7.

following questions.

First, does alcohol help me grow spiritually? If not, then is it wise to consume alcohol at all?

Second, do I experience more of the joy of Jesus when I drink?

Third, am I prone to overindulgence? If so, it would be prudent to refrain from drinking alcohol altogether—just as someone who is prone to overindulgence in gambling should stay far away from casinos.

This section may not apply to you, but learning about the dangers of these diseases can help you to provide support for others.

Alcoholism

The Centers for Disease Control and Prevention defines alcoholism as excessive heavy drinking, defined as eight or more drinks per week for a woman or fifteen or more drinks per week for a man. So we're not talking about an occasional glass of wine. Alcoholism destroys families, and the occasional glass of wine does not.

This is alcoholism:

> As the cold, damp wet awakens me, I'm puzzled as to what has happened. My clothes are drenched with sweat and the stench of vomit—a constant reminder of how sick this problem has made me. The smell of vomit hits my nostrils as if I had just walked across a landfill. The memory of the evening before is foggy. As much as I try to remember, I can't!
>
> It's early morning and I'm again awakened by the familiar taunting of the demon that's wearing on me. Slowly, I pull myself out of bed and go to the kitchen cabinet, where I keep the bottle of gin. I take a swig from the bottle and consider the insanity of the situation: the burning sensation is strangely enjoyable as it goes down

my throat. The excitement comes as I tiptoe back to my room, realizing that, soon, I will get that much-needed sleep.

The morning brings the same life-numbing routine: get up and drink, go to work and drink, go to lunch and drink, and come home and drink until bedtime. In my rational moments, I remember how it all started. But always the alcohol and pills keep my recovery at a distance, as a mantra in my mind. I say over and over, "I need to quit..."

The protocol for recovery from alcohol is to medically detox at a licensed facility. If you drink daily and your alcohol consumption has increased, then you have a problem. You can't just stop on your own. You need professional help.

After detox, your recovery plan should follow these steps:

1. Daily on your knees ask God to take the desire to drink away.
2. Ask God to keep you sober for today.
3. Read Scripture alone and with your family.
4. Obtain a Christian sponsor.
5. Attend a support group.
6. Attend counseling.
7. Develop a routine that does not involve alcohol.
8. Develop a negative image of the past problems that alcohol has caused in your life.
9. Develop positive images that your new abstinence has afforded you.
10. Thank God at bedtime for keeping you sober today.

Question:

Do you have a husband or wife who you feel drinks too much? If so, then now is the time to discuss this issue. Write down why you think there may be a drinking problem.

Opioid Addiction

An opioid is a substance used to treat moderate-to-severe pain. It is highly addictive when used frequently. The Centers for Disease Control and Prevention reported on May 1, 2022, that there had been more than 100,000 overdose deaths in the previous twelve months. Indeed, opioid abuse is the number one addiction among young people today.

This addiction often starts with someone having severe pain from an injury or surgery. The physician prescribes an opioid for pain management. The patient can become innocently addicted without even trying. What is not common knowledge is that a user can build a tolerance to the drug and end up always needing more to achieve pain relief or to maintain the addiction. Then the user ends up going outside the normal office visit to obtain their drug—frequenting other medical providers or buying drugs off the street. Again, the spouse of the addicted person ends up having a relationship with the drug instead of the person they are married to. In addition, obtaining drugs to maintain the habit becomes extremely expensive.

A wellness protocol for the opioid addict starts with detox with a physician on an outpatient basis—unless it would be physically dangerous for you, then have a physician admit you to the detox unit of a medical facility. After detox, the steps for recovery are as follows:

1. Daily Bible reading.
2. Daily prayer.
3. A Christian support system.
4. A Christian sponsor.
5. Develop a negative image of what addiction did to you and your family.
6. Develop positive images of how your life has been since getting into recovery.
7. Attend church and volunteer in some capacity.

Gambling Addiction

Gambling addiction has increased since the availability of online poker and sports betting. Nothing will take a family's money faster than these two games. When there is a gambling addict in the family, someone else in the family should manage the money. The gambler should never carry much money or a family credit card—they should agree to a minimum daily allotment for food, gas, and work expenses. They should not receive more than that amount. Money is a cue for gambling.

The recovery protocol for a gambling addict includes the following:

1. Stay out of casinos.
2. Don't use the computer to enter any online gambling sites.
3. Join a gambling support group.
4. Sit down weekly with your spouse to account for your spending.
5. Read Scripture daily and pray that the Lord takes away the desire to gamble.
6. Carry very little money.
7. If sports betting is a problem, you may have to stop watching games for a time.

Sexual Addiction

Sexual addiction has been on the rise since the advent of the Internet. The internet has made access to pornography much easier. Years ago, one had to walk to the nearest newsstand and purchase a pornographic magazine in public. Online viewing is much more explicit than in magazines.

This is an addiction that robs a couple of normal experiences in the marriage bed. Just as Adam and Eve tried to hide from God after committing a sin against God, we often try to hide when we sin. Sin leads to hiding what we have done for fear of being found out. In the context of sexual addiction, hiding our sin can involve the frequent erasing of pornographic websites on the internet history, or hiding purchases of pornographic magazines or prostitutes to feed our sexual addiction.

Pornography is anything that we use for sexual stimulation or self-gratification, whether it was designed for that purpose or not.[43] Any sin—whether viewing pornography or something else—brings temporary pleasure, but it is guaranteed to bring shame, followed by a strategy to hide the sin. It is interesting that the rest of the Biblical story after Genesis 3 explains that humanity has closed eyes in terms of their spiritual condition and needs God to open their eyes so they can be born again through faith in Jesus.[44] This means the answer to any addiction is a relationship with God through His Son, Jesus. Only God has the power to break the chains of addiction in our lives.

The sex addict soon becomes uninterested in a familiar partner. He or she would rather have sex with a stranger. The sex addict also cannot get excited about normal sex, because the addiction requires abnormal sexual practices. Physical hook-ups (which often begin online) put the spouse who is not addicted in harm's way, raising the possibility that they may get a sexually transmitted disease. The addict may use money that belongs to the family on prostitutes as well, putting the family finances in jeopardy.

Sexual addiction is the most difficult to stop due to the biological aspects of the sex drive. The sex drive is as strong as the craving for food and water. But sexual addiction has a progression that ultimately leads to devastation.

The good news is that it is possible to intervene early enough to stop this. Young men and women in their teens have a curiosity about sex, especially during their puberty years. Internet pornography has taken advantage of this curiosity. Parents can and should intervene in their

---

43. Tim Chester, *Closing the Window* (Downers Grove: IVP Books, 2010), 8.

44. Andrew Steinmann, *Genesis*, vol. 1 (Downers Grove: 2019), 69.

children's lives earlier so that the addiction doesn't take hold, giving them an unhealthy view of God's gift of sexuality, which was designed to be used in the confines of marriage.[45]

Sexual sin appears enticing, at least on the surface. It appeals to our sinful fleshly desires and our longing to satisfy the urges. The former King of Israel, Solomon, knew too well about sexual desire. He had 700 wives and 300 concubines who negatively impacted his life spiritually.[46] In Proverbs 5, Solomon wrote to his son instructing him to stay far away from the "strange" or "forbidden" woman. The forbidden woman is the adulteress, who is not his son's wife. She possessed seductive speech—Solomon said her lips dripped with honey and her speech was smoother than oil (verse 3). Note that there is an intrinsic and inseparable connection between speech and sex.[47] Adulterous affairs are rarely based *solely* on physical attraction.

Affairs involve affirmation communicated from the woman to the man and there has been a willing listener and encouraging man who has caught the attention, especially emotionally, of another woman. Affairs often arise because the guilty party discovers another person who meets an unmet need in his or her life.

When that need is met—whether it is kind words, a listening ear, or empathy—attraction is born, and an affair is a likely result. In Proverbs 5, it is the woman who entices the man with speech, but in our day, it could

---

45. One practical way of parents shepherding their children through the teenage years is for fathers to read through a book together with their son or mothers to read a book together with their daughters and discuss. Books have a way of surfacing issues and promoting discussion that might not otherwise occur. Two book suggestions are *Every Man's Battle: Winning the War on Sexual Temptation One Victory at a Time* by Stephen Arterburn and Fred Stoeker or the female version is *Every Woman's Battle* by Shannon Ethridge and Stephen Arterburn. A second recommended book is *Unwanted: How Sexual Brokenness Reveals Our Way to Healing* by Jay Stringer.

45. See 1 Kings 11:3; "He had 700 wives, who were princesses, and 300 concubines. And his wives turned away his heart."

47. Bruce K. Waltke, *The Book of Proverbs*, vol. 1 (Grand Rapids: Eerdmans, 2004), 308.

just as easily be the man who seduces another woman through romantic poems, love songs, and empty promises.

Wellness protocol for the sex addict:

1. Christians will need to die daily to themselves and allow Jesus to help them one day at a time. We can wake up each day and pray that the Lord will work through us to conquer the sexual desires that keep us defeated in our everyday lives—especially our marriages.

2. Daily use of negative/positive imaging is recommended. Write down and create several negative images that have happened to you while actively involved in your sexual addiction. For example, your credit card balance is huge due to online porn charges. Practice thinking about these negative images when triggered to act out sexually. The negative image will become an involuntary response that your mind continues to implement daily in your thoughts to override the desire to relapse.

3. Write down positive images created since you've been in recovery. Remember them and set goals around them to reinforce success. Remember: one relapse will have you starting all over again. All the good that's happened during your recovery will be wiped out. Positive imagery can help you avoid this. For example, you have more money now that you're not spending it on call girls or at the topless bars. You're spending more quality time with the family.

4. Ask God daily to remove the desire for abnormal sex and create a desire to have pleasurable sex with your spouse.

5. Read a verse of Scripture daily and use that as a mantra in your comings and goings for that day. Make it a part of

your inner thoughts.

6. Ask friends—or a Christian sponsor who understands what you're going through—to accept a phone call from you or meet with you when you're having triggers that can lead to relapse.

7. Avoid people, places, and things that trigger you. You know what those things are and may want to journal them to reinforce your negative image.

8. Don't keep secrets, especially regarding temptation. If there's been forgiveness in your marriage, then ask your wife or husband if it's okay to be transparent with them. If it's not okay, then honor their boundaries.

9. Seek a counselor who has experience in sex addiction. Perhaps seek out a Christian counselor who specializes in sex therapy with couples. Your sexual health has been compromised, and your marriage's sexual health has been damaged. The marriage bed will need repairing and a slow approach to regain sexual pleasure in your relationship so the injured party can build trust again.

In any addiction, a Christian will experience spiritual darkness. This is not to be confused with depression (psychological darkness); it is, rather, *total* darkness, involving a break in communication with the Lord. For a Christian, this is a dangerous and uncomfortable place, due to the difficulty of getting fellowship back with the Lord. After sexually acting out, staying in recovery is the way back to peace and light.

As a Christian, the ultimate negative image is the daily darkness that overtakes your life in the wake of your addiction. Say to yourself, "I don't want to grieve the Holy Spirit. I want an intimate and sweet relationship with my Lord and Savior Jesus Christ."

Remember the times you were in spiritual darkness, separated from God, your fellowship with Him broken. When the desire to relapse comes, then immediately go to these negative images, to maintain your strength against temptations.

Every day, look at the progress you've made by writing in your journal—describe the process of being in remission from sexual addiction (or, for that matter, any addictions). Remember that the positive things that have happened in your life due to your ongoing recovery would be wiped out with one relapse. A sex addict's daily mantra can be, "My addiction was my bondage, but my recovery is my freedom."

Finally, what story do you want to be told about you one day at your funeral? Do you want your addiction to be part of your legacy? Remember, there are only two ways out of addiction: jail or death.

JOURNALING PAGES

Journal your thoughts and revelations from Chapter 8

Chapter 9:
Financial Freedom

Now that we've looked at some of the ways the enemy can steal your family's money, let's look at ways God can have you build a strong financial foundation for your family. Calculate how much money you've spent on addictions or overspending. Tighten up and save! If your church offers a Dave Ramsey course or other series on finances, consider attending. Ramsey's series has helped many people achieve financial freedom.

Every Christian needs to discuss tithing. God has said to test Him by giving a percentage of money to Him.[48] Follow Ramsey's rules for saving and spending. Also, look at these steps to financial freedom:

1. Decide as a family how much money you can put away after each paycheck, even if it's just a few dollars. Couples should discuss what they each spend money on daily, even

---

48. See Malachi 3:10; "Bring the full tithe into the storehouse, that there may be food in my house. And thereby put me to the test, says the LORD of hosts, if I will not open the windows of heaven for you and pour down for you a blessing until there is no more need."

if it's just a Starbucks coffee or some other drink. Decide together what you can give up and put into savings.

2. Work to eliminate credit card debt.

3. Give money to your church. The Lord asks you to test Him on this. See the verse of scripture in Malachi 3:10.

4. If your company has a 401K savings plan, participate in it. Not participating is like leaving money on the table; this is money you should earmark for saving.

5. If your company doesn't provide a savings plan, contact your local banker for information and help in saving.

6. After your debt has been eliminated, pay extra amounts on your home. Living in a debt-free home can free you to be generous in radical ways.

The class could also invite a financial planner who is a church member or a professional financial planner from the community to speak on this subject. This can help motivate a young couple to start planning a financial future together. Often a couple thinks they have to make a lot of money in order to start saving, but in reality, saving can be as simple as giving up spending on something you can do without, and instead putting that money into a savings account.

Write a plan that you and your spouse can live with to achieve financial health.

Please remember, you are running a small family business where financial success or failure can determine the outcome for everyone. Financial problems are one of the leading causes of divorce, in addition to all the above-mentioned problems.

In closing, this course has taken you into a deeper understanding of the problems that can destroy a marriage and break up a family. We feel that although some of these issues are uncomfortable to work through, it is necessary to expose them to achieve a healthier family life. May God bless your family going forward by keeping these practices ongoing.

A checklist for ending each day:

1. Read Scripture daily. Do this together, possibly before bedtime.

2. Individually read one verse of Scripture and carry it in your mind to think about throughout the day.

3. Be affectionate with one another daily.

4. Always before leaving the house or hanging up a phone call, say, "I love you" to your spouse.

5. Discuss problems immediately when they arise. Remember, you are running a family business and your actions affect the success or failure of that business.

6. Do not keep secrets.

7. Stay sexually active within the marriage.

8. Discuss your financial health and ways you can improve it.

9. Work on ways you can individually stay healthy physically and mentally.

10. Be slow to anger. Be kind.

JOURNALING PAGE